Cactus Hotel

Henry Holt and Company, LLC, *Publishers since 1866*
175 Fifth Avenue, New York, New York 10010
www.henryholtchildrensbooks.com

Distributed in Canada by H. B. Fenn and Company Ltd.

Library of Congress Cataloging-in-Publication Data
Guiberson, Brenda.
Cactus hotel / Brenda Guiberson; illustrated by Megan Lloyd.
Summary: Describes the life cycle of the giant saguaro cactus,
with an emphasis on its role as a home for other desert dwellers.
1. Saguaro—Juvenile literature. 2. Desert ecology—Sonoran Desert—
Juvenile literature. [1. Saguaro. 2. Cactus. 3. Desert ecology. 4. Ecology.]
I. Lloyd, Megan, ill. II. Title.
QK495.C11G85 1991 574.5'2652—dc20 90-41748

ISBN-13: 978-0-8050-1333-7 / ISBN-10: 0-8050-1333-4 (hardcover)
25 24 23 22 21 20 19
ISBN-13: 978-0-8050-2960-4 / ISBN-10: 0-8050-2960-5 (paperback)
30 29 28 27 26 25
First published in hardcover in 1991 by Henry Holt and Company
First paperback edition—1993
Manufactured in China

For my mother and father, and the whole Zangar clan —B.G.

To Carol, thanks for the music —M.L.L.

CACTUS HOTEL

Brenda Z. Guiberson
Illustrated by Megan Lloyd

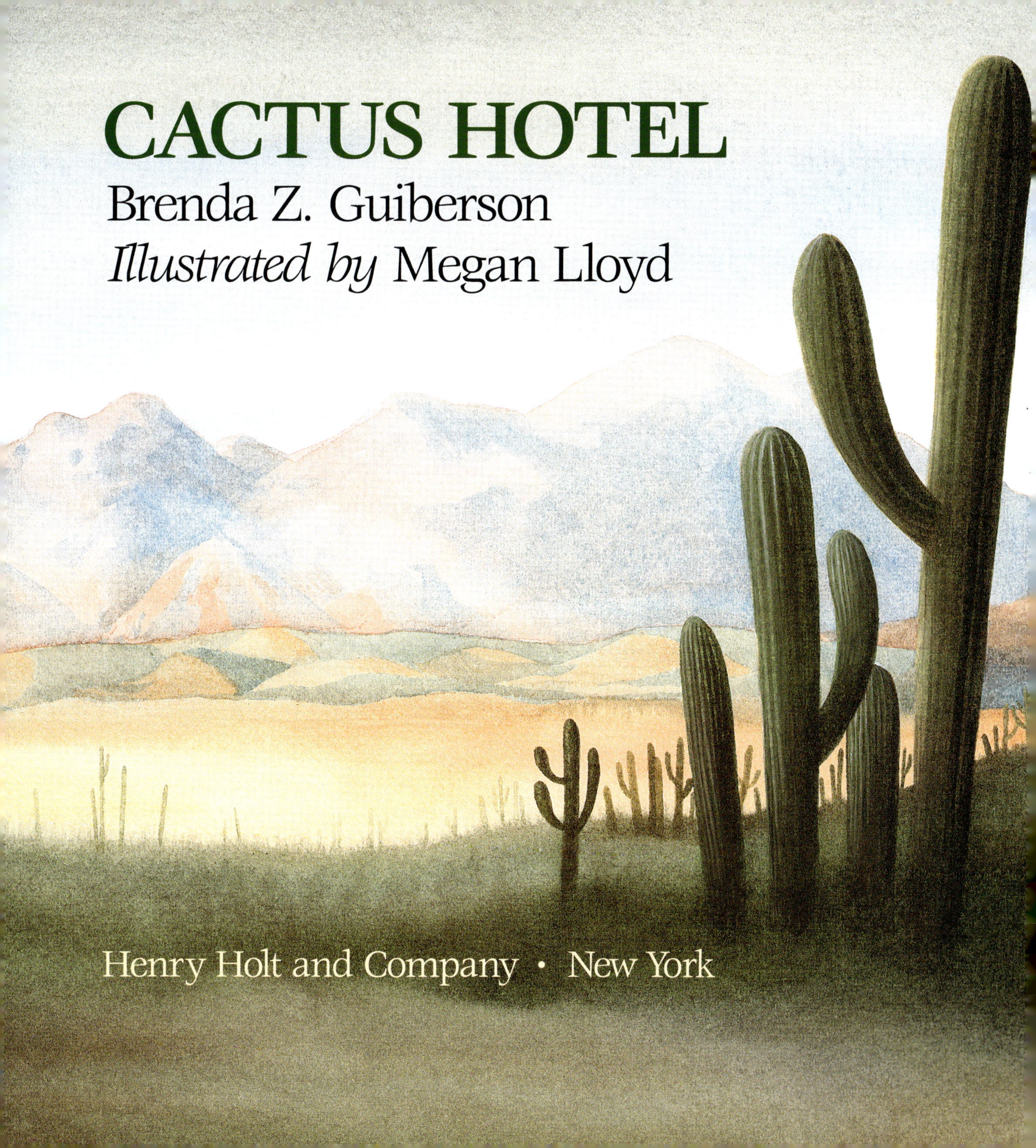

Henry Holt and Company • New York

On a hot, dry day in the desert, a bright-red fruit falls from a tall saguaro cactus. *Plop.* It splits apart on the sandy floor. Two thousand black seeds glisten in the sunlight.

When the air cools in the evening, an old pack rat comes out and eats the juicy fruit. Then he skitters across the sand. A seed left clinging to his whiskers falls off under a palo-verde tree.

It is a good place for the seed to drop. A spotted ground squirrel looking for something to eat does not see it. A house finch chirping high in the paloverde does not see it.

After many dry days, a heavy rain falls on the desert. Soon a young cactus sprouts up from the ground.

Slowly, slowly the seedling grows. The paloverde protects it from the hot summer sun and cold winter nights. After ten years the cactus is only four inches high. It is just big enough for desert ants to climb its spiny sides.

After a rainstorm, when the desert blooms with color, the cactus pulls in water with its long roots and looks fat. A young pack rat stops to drink the water that drips off the tree. Then she scurries off, looking for a dry place to make a nest.

When there is no rain, the cactus uses up the water it has stored inside and looks thin. The paloverde loses its tiny leaves. But there is always some shade for the cactus below. After twenty-five years, the cactus is two feet tall. A jackrabbit cools off beside it and gnaws on the green pulp. But when a coyote moves in the distance, the jackrabbit disappears into a nearby hole.

After fifty years the cactus stands ten feet tall and looks straight and strong beside the old paloverde. For the very first time, brilliant white-and-yellow flowers appear at the top of the cactus. Every spring from now on, the flowers will open for

one night only and then close in the heat of the day. They beckon like a welcoming signal across the desert. At different times of the day and night birds, bees, and bats come for the nectar.

The flowers dry up, and after a month the bright-red fruit filled with black seeds is ripe and ready. A Gila woodpecker comes to eat. He looks around the cactus and decides to stay.

He has found the perfect place in the desert to begin a new hotel.

The woodpecker goes right to work, and the only tool he uses is his long, hard beak. *Tap, tap, tap.* He bores into the flesh of the cactus. *Tap, tap, tap.* He digs deep inside, to make a space that is comfortable and roomy.

The cactus is not harmed. It forms a tough scab all around the hole to protect itself from drying out. The woodpecker gets a weatherproof nest that is shady on hot days, and warm and insulated on frosty nights. And the cactus gets something in return: The woodpecker likes to eat the insects that can bring disease to the cactus.

After sixty years the cactus hotel is eighteen feet tall. To add more space, it begins to grow an arm. A woodpecker has a new hole in the trunk. Farther up, a white-winged dove makes a nest on the arm. And down below, an old hole is discovered by an elf owl. The birds feel safe, living high up in a prickly plant where nothing can reach them.

All around the desert there are holes of every size, for ants and mice, lizards and snakes, rabbits and foxes. After a hundred and fifty years, there are holes of every size in the cactus, too. The giant plant has finally stopped growing. It is fifty feet tall, with seven long branches. It weighs eight tons—about as much as five automobiles.

Everybody wants to live in the cactus hotel. Birds lay eggs and pack rats raise their young. Even insects and bats live there.

When one animal moves out, another moves in. And every spring they come for a special treat of nectar and juicy red fruit.

Finally, after two hundred years, the old cactus sways in a gust of wind and falls with a thud to the sandy floor. Its great thorny arms crumble in the crash.

The creatures that lived up high must find other homes. But those that prefer to live down low move right in. A millipede, a scorpion, and many ants and termites quickly find homes in the toppled hotel.

After many months, all that remains are the wooden ribs that supported the cactus while it stood so tall. A collared lizard dashes over the top, looking for insects. A ground snake huddles in the shade below.

And all around, there is a forest of cacti slowly, slowly growing in the desert. Through hot and cold, wet and dry, some will survive long enough to become other cactus hotels.

The saguaro [suh-WAH-ruh *or* suh-GWA-row] cactus can be found only in the Sonoran Desert of southern Arizona and northern Mexico. A sign identifies a large area of these plants as a Saguaro Forest. A forest? If this is a forest, where are the leaves?

The saguaro does not have leaves. A tree with broad leaves can lose a hundred gallons of water in a day. But a cactus has adapted its shape and tissues so that it loses less than one glass of water a day. The saguaro hoards water, and uses the moisture stored inside during the long dry periods of the desert. On rare occasions, after a rainstorm, a saguaro will take in too much water, and a section will burst. Usually the cactus is able to heal over the injury and recover.

Does this leafless plant have any wood? The long, straight rods inside the cactus are the wood. Human desert dwellers have always valued this material for building. It makes good roofs, fences, and fuel. It is also useful for reaching the fruit at the top of the giant cactus. The saguaro fruit was so important to the local Papago Indians that they began their calendar year with the time of the fruit harvest.

Today a large saguaro is prized so much for landscape reasons that "cactus rustlers" receive thousands of dollars to illegally uproot and deliver large specimens. Saguaros that have grown to old age have survived droughts, freezes, flash floods, brush fires, and high concentrations of pack rats, which eat the seedlings. Without saguaros, there would be a severe shortage of food and nesting sites for creatures of the desert.